Glendale College
Library

MATHEMATICS
FOR THE YOUNG CHILD

THE EARLY CHILDHOOD ACTIVITIES SERIES

▮ MATHEMATICS
FOR THE YOUNG CHILD

SARA THROOP   Youngstown State University, Youngstown, Ohio

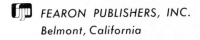 *FEARON PUBLISHERS, INC.*
Belmont, California

Editor: Lesley Anne Swanson
Designer: Eleanor Mennick
Illustrator: Claudia Ricketts

ISBN-0-8224-4425-9

Printed in the United States of America.

6/76

CONTENTS

4 VOCABULARY 33

Where is the other part? How big is it? Which is largest? How much water is there? Is it too heavy to lift? Which picture comes first? What is a circle? What is a triangle? What is a square? I'm thinking of a shape. Are the birds standing on circles? Are these shoes the same? Who has more? Who's *both*? Can we have more cookies? Will it go fast? Where do we play baseball? What's inside the ball? Are there enough napkins? Is my hair longer than Tammy's?

5 COUNTING 48

Do you have three feet? How many stars do you have? One, two, buckle my shoe. How many tricycles do we have? How many wheels can you count? Which pile has three? How old are you? How many feet does an elephant have? How many windows do you see? Which hands match? How many legs do you have? Can you show me how many with your fingers? Who has three crayons? Who can count to five? How many are twins? What comes in pairs? How many cookies do we need? How many people are there in your family? How much money is it? Do these match? How many clothespins are there? Are there as many houses as trees? Let's play store!

PREFACE

Mathematics is exciting for young children because it gives them new tools to work with. After you have presented an exercise from this book, you will note the children applying the new words and ideas to many other situations. The way you use these pages will vary, for you and the children you work with are unique.

Nondirected classroom activities will often indicate readiness for a particular activity. When you hear two children arguing "Mine is bigger" and "No, *mine* is bigger," you know they are ready for more activities with words comparing size.

Be sure to write in this book. Put stars beside the activities you enjoyed. Write down that astute observation one child made. Note changes you would like to make the next time. These exercises will become more valuable to you the more you use them.

Pick up this book when you wonder, "What would be fun to do today?" Have fun yourself. If you enjoy learning, the children will share your enthusiasm.

MATHEMATICS
FOR THE YOUNG CHILD

MAKING COMPARISONS

Learning Objective: To help the children develop an awareness of comparative size, quantity, monetary value, and speed.

WHO IS TALLER THAN LAURIE?

Equipment. An oversized, colorful meter stick; chart for recording each child's height.

Procedure. ASK: Do you know anyone who is shorter than you are? Do you know anyone who is taller than you? Who is shorter? Who is taller? Are some of you here today about the same size? How can you tell who is taller? Can you measure by standing next to each other?

SAY: Let's compare height on the meter stick. Each of you can stand against this measuring chart on the wall, and I'll write your name on it. Then you can see how tall you are.

When everyone has been measured, ask: Can you tell who is taller than you? Here is Laurie's name. Who is taller than she is? Is everyone taller than Laurie? Who is taller than David? His name is at the top of the chart. Am I taller than David?

You might also hold up pictures from children's books and have the children identify the taller person on a given page.

To the Teacher. Children are aware of their own height and the heights of others in their family. They can easily see that Mom is taller than they, or that they are taller than a brother or sister. Encourage and reinforce this ability to compare height visually.

As you introduce the measurements on the chart, the children will begin to perceive height in a slightly different manner than they did before. Together, compare objects as well as people—buildings, bushes, flowers, chairs.

WHICH TRUCK IS LONGER?

Equipment. Blocks and toy cars of various sizes; a meter stick.

Procedure. SAY: Let's each choose a block and place it next to someone else's block in a row. Now we have pairs of blocks. Jason, is the block you put down shorter or longer than the one Lisa put next to it? Look closely and pick up the one that is longer.

Have each child choose the longer block of a pair of blocks, then say: Here are some toy cars and trucks. I'm going to arrange the cars and trucks in groups of two. Can you tell me which one is longer? Allow each child to pick the longer toy from a pair.

SAY: These toys are close in size. Let's see if we can tell which one is longer by putting each one on this meter stick. Which one is longer? Which one takes up more space on the meter stick? It is longer.

To the Teacher. The comparison of length involves basically the same concepts as the comparison of height. In fact, some objects can be measured by both height and length, depending on whether they are positioned horizontally or vertically. For example, have two children lie side by side on the floor and determine who is longer. Then have them stand to compare height.

In this activity, the meter stick is horizontal as toys are placed on it to be measured. Show how it resembles the vertical stick used to measure height. The children now should be able to talk in terms of both height and length. Encourage them to compare other things in this manner.

WHOSE FOOT IS SHORTER?

Equipment. Strips of paper of various lengths; meter stick, chalk.

Procedure. SAY: Let's play a game with our feet. Joey, you and Harold each put one of your shoes together. Who has the shorter foot? Have these children then compare length of feet with the other children in the class. ASK: Are your feet longer than some and shorter than others? Does anyone have feet the same size as yours?

Pass out the paper. SAY: I'm giving each of you a strip of paper. Can you find someone whose strip of paper is shorter than yours? How can you tell which is longer and which is shorter? Is your paper longer than some and shorter than others? Mark with chalk where your piece of paper comes on this meter stick. Whose paper is the longest? Whose is the shortest?

To the Teacher. With a variety of experiences like this one, reinforce the child's concept of longer and shorter. Encourage the children to use this concept as they draw, build, and compare things: Whose hair is longer? Which table is longer? Which car is longer? The more the children apply these terms, the better they grasp these concepts.

WHICH ONE IS BIGGER?

Equipment. A piece of paper, folded in half, for each child; a crayon for each child.

Procedure. Ask: Let's talk about the difference between *smaller* and *bigger*. Joan, is your hand smaller, or bigger than my hand? Eric, is this book smaller, or bigger than that book?

Say: I have a piece of paper for each of you. Here is something to draw with. Now I want each of you to decide what you want to make on your paper. Whatever you choose, you will draw two of them. You might want to draw two eggs, or two faces, or two dogs. You must be very careful, though, because I want you to make one thing big and the other thing small. Here is my paper. See that I have made one big ball and one small ball. Both of my pictures are of balls, but on this half I drew a big ball, and on this half I drew a small one.

Help the children as they choose and draw small and big objects. When they are finished, ask them to trade papers with one another. When they have someone else's paper, ask each to put an *X* below the bigger item.

To the Teacher. The children have all identified smaller and bigger things by touching and comparing. This activity requires them not only to identify but to create things that illustrate these concepts.

WHICH EGG CARTON HAS MORE EGGS?

Equipment. Several regular egg cartons, a few half-dozen cartons, plastic eggs in several colors.

Procedure. Ask: Can anyone tell me what you buy in these cartons? Is this carton full? Hold up a full-dozen carton with 12 eggs. Say: Now I'm going to move these eggs. I'll put these green ones where the red ones were. How many eggs are there now? Even though I changed them around, there are still the same number, aren't there?

Hold up a half-dozen carton and say: This egg carton is smaller than the first one. How many eggs are in it? Is it full? Let's empty the big carton and put these eggs in it. Now how many eggs are there? Is the carton full? Are there as many as there were at first?

Now let's fill another small carton with eggs. Is the carton full now? If we put these eggs with the others in the big carton, will they all fit? Now the carton is full again. There are enough eggs to fill the bigger carton.

To the Teacher. Although many children can recite numbers, their concept of these numbers may not be meaningful. The children will be able to see, however, that if all the holes in the egg carton are full there are the same number of eggs, no matter how they rearrange them. Using the smaller number of eggs shows that the number is the same no matter what container it is in. Do not deal here with the numerals 1 to 6 or 1 to 12, but simply with the idea that the number remains the same despite the fact the positions of the objects may be changed.

WHO IS OLDER?

Equipment. Pictures of people of various ages.

Procedure. ASK: How old are you? Did you just have a birthday? Do you have a birthday coming soon? Do you have any brothers or sisters? Are you older than they? Are they older than you? Is your mom older than you? How can you tell? Is your grandfather older than your dad? Do you know someone older than you who is not as tall as you are?

SAY: Let's look at some pictures of people. Can you tell who is older in this one? How do you know the mother is older than the girl? Is it sometimes hard to tell who is older? Look at these boys. Could they be about the same age?

To the Teacher. Children are extremely age conscious and often can't wait to be older. Help them understand and be able to recognize obvious age differences. Point out that graying hair and wrinkled skin are often clues to an older age, and that size can often, but not always, help indicate who is older.

WHO CAN REMEMBER?

Equipment. Pairs of small items that illustrate *longer* and *shorter,* such as: long straw, short straw; long block, short block; long pencil, short pencil.

Procedure. Today we're going to play a game about long and short. Ask: Do you remember what these words mean? Is the table in our room longer or shorter than the room? Is the meter stick longer or shorter than the wall?

Say: This is a remembering game. I'm going to show you two things. Look at them carefully and decide which is shorter and which is longer, but don't say a word. Just decide and be very quiet. After you've looked at these things, I'll put them behind my back and ask one of you to tell me which one is shorter, or longer.

Hold up the two straws. Remind the children to study them in silence. Put these items behind your back, then ask: Who can remember which hand has the shorter straw? Call on a child to answer. Ask the others if they agree. Bring both items into view again and compare them verbally and by touching.

Continue the game using other objects. Give each child a chance to identify the shorter or longer member of a pair.

To the Teacher. The children have been comparing objects by touch and measurement. This activity challenges them to compare by sight alone with the additional requirement that they remember once they have compared. Start out with obvious examples and gradually progress to more complicated ones.

WHICH TREE HAS MORE LEAVES?

Equipment. Two plants—one with few leaves, one with many; pictures on the chalkboard of two trees with different numbers of leaves; three toy cars, five blocks, seven pencils.

Procedure. Say: Here are two plants. Can anyone tell me which plant has more leaves? How can you tell? Do you have to count the leaves or can you tell by looking? Look at these trees I've drawn on the chalkboard. Which one has more leaves? How can you tell? Did you need to count? How many does this one have? How many leaves does the other one have?

Here are some cars and some blocks. Are there more blocks than cars? How many cars are there? How many blocks? Are there more pencils here than there are cars? Are there more pencils than blocks? Do you need to count to find out?

To the Teacher. Most children know and use the word *more,* as in "He has more cookies than I have." Have the children match blocks and cars, for example, to demonstrate that there are more blocks than cars. Some children can count to ten but do not understand that seven is more than three.

IS ONE SHOE ENOUGH?

Equipment. A shoe, a glove, a boot, a sock; pictures of shoes in groups of two or one; pictures of children, one for each child.

Procedure. SAY: You have seen all these things before. Can you tell me what each of these is used for?

Hold up a shoe. ASK: Is one shoe enough? Why not? Why do we need two shoes? How many feet do people have? Why do we need two socks? Two boots?

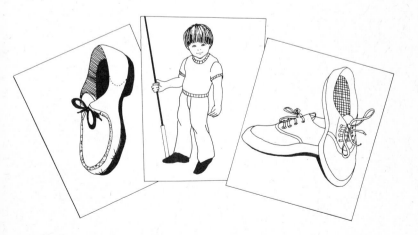

How many hands do you have? Is one glove enough? Why not? Why do you need two gloves?

Give each child a picture of a child, and place the pictures of shoes in a pile. Ask the children to find a picture that has enough shoes for the child's feet. Be sure that some pictures have one shoe and some have two.

To the Teacher. The children should have little difficulty in grasping this concept, but probably have never thought about it objectively. They all wear shoes and gloves or mittens, so they will be able to relate to comparing this ratio of 2:1.

CAN WE ALL SIT DOWN?

Equipment. Chairs arranged in a circle with one for each child; record player and record.

Procedure. Ask: Have you ever played musical chairs? It's a game we play with chairs and music. We'll all walk around the chairs while the music plays, and when the music stops, you sit down. Are you ready?

Let the record play for 10 or 15 seconds, then turn it off. Say: Now the music has stopped. Can we all sit down? Are there enough chairs? Yes. Now when we march around again, I'll take away one chair. Someone won't have a chair.

Play the music again, removing one chair. When it stops, say: Someone is left standing. Chris, will you stand here with me while the music starts again? Have Chris help you remove a chair before the music stops again, and procede with the questions as before.

Continue to have the children who do not have chairs help you remove a chair each time. End the game when just one child is left.

To the Teacher. The children can tell by looking that someone is left out; there are not enough chairs. As the game progresses, have them count people and chairs and try to decide whether there will be enough chairs. Ask: Are there more chairs or more people? This is a game children enjoy, and it can be used to reinforce their concept of comparison.

IS THERE A CUP FOR EACH ONE?

Equipment. A cup for each child for a drink at lunch or snack time; an equal number of straws or popsicle sticks.

Procedure. SAY: It's time for our snack (or lunch) now. Each place at the table is set with a cup. Is there a cup for each of us? How can we find out?

Listen to their answers and, if possible, use the children's suggestions for comparing cups and children. They may suggest counting. If so, have each child choose a place to sit. ASK: Can we tell now if there is a cup for each one? How can we tell? Does each person have a cup? Were there enough? Were any left over?

Place a few straws or popsicle sticks on the table and ask if there is one for each child. ASK: Is it easy to tell? Does it look like enough? Add more straws so there is one for each child, then ask again if there are enough. ASK: How can we tell if there are enough? Each of you take a straw and let's see if there are enough.

To the Teacher. If you attempt to prove by counting that there are enough drinks, you may convince the children only partially, as the numbers have little meaning for them. By comparing cups to people, however, they can see there are enough. The pile of straws will be more difficult to estimate, but as each child takes one they can see there are enough.

CAN WE ALL HAVE A DRINK?

Equipment. Pitcher with some juice in it; a cup for each child.

Procedure. ASK: Is there enough juice here to fill your cup, Barry? Yes, there is. There is a lot of juice in the pitcher, but do you think there is enough for everyone? How can we tell?

Pour some juice into each child's cup, then ask: Was the pitcher full before we poured the juice? Is it full now? How much is left? Elicit responses such as a little, half, a lot.

Encourage the children to estimate that there is juice left over, but probably not enough for each one to have another full cup. Someone may suggest that there might be enough to go around if everyone has a little bit, rather than a full cup. Try this, and help the children draw the conclusion that this way, there is enough.

To the Teacher. It will be difficult for the children to estimate the amount of water in the pitcher. Even adults misjudge quantities a container can hold because the shape is often deceptive.

WHO RAN FASTER?

Equipment. Toy cars; START and FINISH lines taped on the floor; pictures of a car, a horse-drawn buggy, a plane, a train, a bicycle, and a boat.

Procedure. ASK: Do you like to run fast? Is it fun to have races? Let's see who can run faster today, Scott or Donny. Pair all the children for short foot races and let them see who ran faster today.

ASK: Which of these toy cars will go faster? Can you guess? Let the children compare the toys and estimate their speed. Then race the cars to determine the winner.

Hold up the pictures and say: Here are pictures of things we can ride on. Which will go faster, a bicycle or a train? A boat or a plane? A car or a horse-drawn buggy?

To the Teacher. As the children run foot races in pairs, emphasize that Scott is faster *today*, but Donny might win tomorrow.

When racing the cars, it is best for you to start the cars, as the children may give them unequal shoves.

As you discuss the pictures of vehicles, be patient if the children don't grasp the differences in speed immediately. An airplane may seem big, but not fast. Perhaps they have seen fast horses and think a horse is faster than a car.

WHICH TREE IS TALLER?

Equipment. Objects of varying heights in the room and outdoors.

Procedure. ASK: Can everyone see the flagpole outside from this window? Do you think the flagpole is taller or shorter than the big tree at the side of the road? How can we find out which is higher since you don't seem to agree?

SAY: Let's go outside and stand beside the tree and then beside the flagpole. Is it easier to tell now which is taller? Can you see other things we can compare? Encourage the children to ask each other questions, such as: Is the bush higher than the gate? In some cases they can use their bodies or hands to compare height. In other cases, they may be able to decide just by looking.

To the Teacher. Appearances are often deceiving, especially to children. An object in the distance may appear to be much smaller than it actually is. A nearby object may appear larger than one in the distance. Help the children sharpen their comparison and estimation skills by standing close to the objects under observation. This way, they can make a more accurate judgment.

HOW WARM IS IT TODAY?

Equipment. A large thermometer placed outside the building in easy view of the children; a simple chart with five blank thermometers drawn on it; a red crayon.

Procedure. ASK: Have any of you noticed what's hanging outside this window? What is it called? What is a thermometer used for? What does it tell us? Does it tell us what the temperature and weather are like?

SAY: Let's go over to the window and look at the thermometer closely. Look for a red line inside the thermometer. This is the most important part of it. When the red line goes up, that tells us the temperature is warmer—there is *more* heat. When it goes down, the temperature is colder—there is *less* heat.

I have made a chart for us to use as we check the thermometer each day. You can help me fill it in today and each day this week. Then we can tell if there is more heat or less heat outside.

With a red crayon, fill in the first thermometer on the chart to match the one outdoors. The next day, have the children help you decide how much of the thermometer on the chart to fill with red. Discuss whether there is more or less red than the amount filled in the previous day. Continue each day to record the temperature. Encourage the children to use the terms *more, less, longer, shorter,* as they discuss the temperature.

To the Teacher. In order to have a variety of temperature readings, you may need to choose a different time during class each day to read the thermometer. Try having the children guess before they check the temperature whether the red line will be shorter or longer than the previous day. Ask: Is it warmer or colder outside today than it was yesterday?

Fahrenheit, a German scientist, designed the thermometer we are familiar with in 1714. It ranged from 0 to 96 degrees. In 1742, the freezing point and the boiling point were adopted as the ends of the scale, and the scale itself was divided into 100 degrees. This is called the centigrade scale and means "hundred steps."

TIME

Learning Objective: To present to the children the various aspects and connotations of time.

2

WHEN DO WE GO HOME?

Equipment. A poster showing the things done in class each day in the sequence usually followed (juice, rest time, story, toys, for example).

Procedure. SAY: Rita wants to know when we go home. Can we help her understand when it's time? Look at these pictures on the bulletin board. What do they show? Are these the things we do in class each day?

ASK: Which things have we already done today? Have we played with the toys? Have we picked up the toys? Have we listened to a story? Have we had rest time?

What things do we still have to do today? Have we been to the bathroom yet? Have we had our snacks? What happens after snack time? Do we get our coats on then, and go home? How can we answer Rita's question? What have we done? What will we do before we go home?

To the Teacher. Children have difficulty comprehending time and are full of questions about it. Introduce the word *after,* and help the children observe the sequence of activities on the poster. Understanding this term in a practical way, such as in answer to Rita's question, deepens the child's understanding of time.

WHEN IS MY BIRTHDAY?

Equipment. Pictures of the four seasons, arranged in sequence; strips of paper with each child's name and birthday on them. Start with the season the children can recognize as *now*. If it is fall, discuss fall first.

Procedure. Ask: Can anyone tell us what season this is? What is the weather like outside? Is it hot or cool? This is fall. Some of your birthdays will soon be here. Let's put your names on this picture of fall.

What season comes after fall? What happens after all the leaves have fallen? It gets cold, doesn't it? We have winter. Who was born in the winter? Let's put your names on this picture of winter. What do we do in the winter?

After winter, what comes next? Do we have spring? What is the weather like in the spring? Let's put the names of the spring birthdays on this spring picture.

After spring comes summer. Who was born in the summer? Do you like the hot summer days? Let's put the names of those with summer birthdays on the summer picture.

Jan's birthday is in the summer. Can you tell us when that will be? After winter and spring, Jan has his birthday. Karen's birthday is in the spring. Is her birthday before or after Jan's?

To the Teacher. An understanding of the terms *before* and *after* is prerequisite to this activity. As children think of birthdays and the seasons, they will also reinforce their concept of the sequence of seasons.

WHEN WILL I BE GROWN UP?

Equipment. A colorful chart showing twenty blocks of time in squares or bars arranged vertically with number one at the bottom.

Procedure. Ask: Have you ever wondered when you will be grown up? Do you remember when you were not this old?

How old are you now? Some of you are three, some are four, some are five. Look at this picture on the bulletin board. There is a block here for every year old that you are. Let's see how far up the chart you are now.

Fill in blocks one and two completely if all the children are at least two. Then fill in the spaces for three, four, or five to show each child's age.

Ask: How much space is left on the chart? Do you still have a lot of spaces to fill? I'll make a line here to show when you will start to school. Is that very far away? Here is another line that shows when you will finish high school. Is it far away?

To the Teacher. Childhood seems to be a slow-moving period of time for some children, even though they are learning more and growing more than they ever will again. A chart can show them the time they have lived in comparison to the school years to come. They can see that they will spend more time in school than they have already lived.

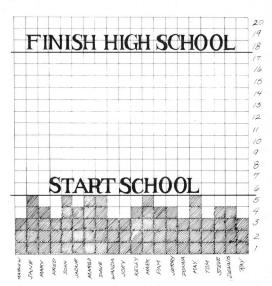

WAS I A BABY ONCE?

Equipment. Pictures of babies and young children.

Procedure. Ask: How old do you think the boy is in this picture? Does he look about your age? What about this girl? Have they always looked this way? Have you always looked as you do now?

What did you look like when you were three (or one year younger than the children are)? Were you as tall as you are now? Did you have as much hair? Were you fatter? Here are some pictures of other children who might be three. Do they look different from a four-year-old?

SAY: Now let's look at some pictures of children who are two. How do these children look different? Do some have diapers on? Are their shoes a different style? Did you ever look like this? Did you wear diapers and hold onto things to walk?

Here is a baby on her first birthday. How does she look different from you? Here are other pictures of one-year-olds. What is different about them?

Have you ever seen a very small baby? What did she look like? Can you imagine you ever looked like that? Have you seen pictures of yourself when you were a baby?

To the Teacher. Most families have some pictures of the children when they were babies. If possible, arrange for a mother to bring a baby to class for the children to see. Talk about babies and how *everyone* was once a baby similar to the ones they've seen. Children have difficulty believing they were ever as small as that because they can't remember this period.

WHEN WILL THERE BE FLOWERS?

Equipment. Seeds for each child to plant or half a sweet potato set on toothpicks in water for each child; paper cups and soil to plant the seeds in; a growth chart.

Procedure. ASK: Have you ever wondered how long it takes a seed like this to grow into a flower? I have a seed here for each of you to plant. Let's each plant one and see how long it takes to grow.

Have each child plant his seed in a cup with his name on it. Allow the children to water the seeds as necessary. Make a chart to show the growing time. Have a child mark off each day on the chart until someone sees a plant coming through the soil (or until the sweet potato starts to sprout). Write each child's name on the calendar the day his seed sprouts.

SAY: Count the number of days it took George's seed to grow. Did it take more days for Karen's to grow? Do you think a tree would grow as fast as a flower? When do we see the most flowers outdoors? When do some of the trees have flowers?

To the Teacher. The study of seeds fits in naturally with the concept of seasons and reinforces the concept of time. Discuss the seasons again, but emphasize the number of days it takes the seed to grow. Help the children understand that some seeds grow to maturity faster than others.

WHEN IS IT MY TURN?

Equipment. Divide the class into groups of two or three for a variety of activities—bean toss, painting, going to the bathroom, playing with a special toy, and so on.

Procedure. SAY: We have many activities going on right now. Henry wants to know when he can have a turn painting. How many are painting today? Henry, three children want to paint. Laura is painting now. You will have a turn after Laura and before Beth.

ASK: Is it sometimes hard to take turns? April and Gary are playing with the bean toss game. April is throwing the bean bags now. Who gets a turn after April? It will be Gary's turn then, won't it?

Continue to discuss taking turns in terms of *before* and *after*. Be sure to keep the groups small.

To the Teacher. Most children are impatient. If you can divide the class into small groups, you can help them to an understanding of *before* and *after* other children. If the entire class is involved, they may become so frustrated that their turn is far away that they fail to concentrate on or grasp these ideas.

WHEN DOES TOMORROW COME?

Equipment. A large calendar, pictures of a sunrise, sunset, and sun at midday; pictures of the moon.

Procedure. ASK: What does tomorrow mean? If I say we are going to the park tomorrow, when would we go to the park? Would we go before or after today?

SAY: Here is a calendar. Will someone make a mark on this square? You have made a mark on today. Now will someone make a mark on this square next to this one? You have made a mark on the square that stands for tomorrow.

How do we know when tomorrow comes? How does each day begin? That's right. The sun comes up and we can see. Here is a picture of the sun coming up in the morning. Then what does the sun do? Here is a picture of the sun high in the sky. When the day ends, what does the sun do? Yes, and here is a picture of the sun setting. Here are some pictures of the moon. When is the moon out?

Tomorrow comes after today. We can tell tomorrow is starting when the sun comes up.

To the Teacher. *Tomorrow* is a confusing concept for a child this age, and it has been said that "tomorrow never comes." The children often hear the term *tomorrow* and need to be helped to understand its relationship to *now*. They are aware of darkness at night and light from the sun, and these ideas can help them realize how tomorrow (or a day) begins and ends. Tomorrow should be described as coming immediately after today, as opposed to a long time from now.

WAS YESTERDAY WHEN I WAS LITTLE?

Equipment. Calendar; reminders of what was done in class yesterday as well as several weeks ago.

Procedure. SAY: This is a calendar that tells what day it is. Will someone put a mark on this square that stands for today? Now let's figure out where yesterday is on the calendar. Is yesterday before or after right now? It's before, isn't it? Paul, will you make a mark on the square before today? This mark shows when yesterday was.

ASK: Can anyone remember what we did in class yesterday? Look around the room for reminders of what we did. Did we read this book? What game did we play? What did we eat at snack time?

Did we make these pictures yesterday? Did we visit the firehouse yesterday? We did these things longer ago than yesterday, didn't we? Were you little yesterday? It was much longer ago than yesterday when you were little.

To the Teacher. Many children associate the term yesterday with the far past and will say they were a baby yesterday, or played in the snow yesterday, when they mean long ago. Help the children realize that yesterday is very close in time to now by recalling activities they did yesterday.

WHEN DO WE EAT?

Equipment. A clock with a second hand in easy view of all the children.

Procedure. SAY: Nearly every day, someone asks me, "When do we eat?" Today, I'd like to show you a way you can tell for yourself when it's time to eat.

Can everyone see the clock? Why do we have clocks? Have you ever asked what time it is? Do you know what time you go to bed at night?

The hands on the clock are moving all the time. Can you see the hand moving? The other hands move also, but we'd have to sit very still for a long time to see these move.

It's time for our snack now. Let's see where the clock hands are now. Which way are they pointing? Tomorrow, when you see the clock like this, can you help me remember it is time for snack?

To the Teacher. Children are generally fascinated by clocks and may come up with some unusual times, such as sixteen o'clock! The clock itself is a mystery to them and too difficult for them to comprehend at this age. It is best, then, to choose one time that can be referred to each day on the clock, such as snack time. Telling time accurately will come later.

WHAT HAPPENED FIRST?

Equipment. Blocks and other toys.

Procedure. ASK: Alice, can you stand in front of Phillip? Where will you stand? If we were making a line, which of you two would be first in line?

The words *in front of* are sometimes hard to use, aren't they? Let's use these blocks to help us figure out what *in front of* means. First I'll put a blue block down, then a red one. Which block did I put down in front of the red one? You're right, the blue one. What do we mean, *in front of*? Did the blue one come first?

Now I'll hand this doll to Carol. Carol, can you give it to Jim? Who touched the doll first? Did Carol touch the doll before Jim? Who else touched the doll before Jim and even before Carol? I touched it before them, didn't I? *Before* is another word that can mean *first* or *in front of*.

To the Teacher. If children find it difficult to comprehend *before* in relation to time, give practice with *before* in relation to position. Give a child who has difficulty three toys or other objects and ask her to place these in various positions: Put the car in front of the wagon. Put the ball in front of the chair. Although the child may use the terms *in front of, first,* and *before,* she will have a better understanding of their exact meanings as she places objects in front of, or stands in front of, or touches something first or before another child.

IS IT TIME TO GET UP?

Equipment. Newspaper, empty milk carton.

Procedure. ASK: Did everyone at your house get up at the same time today? Do you all go to bed at the same time?

Some people go to work or to school at night. Does someone at your house work at night? Why does the milkman go to work so early? When does the newspaper come to your house?

SAY: Let's pretend we are people who work at night. We'll pretend to go to sleep, and Robin will bring the milk to someone. Diane will bring the newspaper.

When the items have been delivered, say: Wake up! It is morning. Who got the milk? Maria, you can be the milkman this time. Terry, you can bring the paper.

To the Teacher. If the children know that delivery trucks, telephone companies, fire stations, and police departments operate twenty-four hours a day, they could act out these roles also.

WHY DO WE NEED CLOCKS?

Equipment. A clock; an egg timer (hour glass); a new toy or special activity.

Procedure. ASK: What does it mean when your mom says, "It's time for bed"? How does your mom know what time it is? Does she tell time from a clock or a watch? Do you know someone else who has a watch or a clock? Does she use it to get you up? Do people use clocks to know when they should go to work?

Hold up the hour glass and ask: Does anyone know what this is? Does your mother have one? What do you think is inside it? That is sand. It was measured very carefully, so that when all the sand goes from one end to the other, a certain amount of time has passed. This amount of sand measures three minutes.

Explain that people used hour glasses before there were clocks. ASK: Why are clocks and watches easier to use? Would it be hard to carry an hour glass with you everywhere? Would it fit in a pocket? Could it break? Might you forget to turn it over when the sand goes down?

Try using the hour glass to settle classroom disputes over the use of special toys. Allow each child to play with the toy until the sand runs down, then the next person takes a turn. This way, they can all see when Joe's turn is over.

To the Teacher. Primitive man measured time by nature—light and darkness and the passage of seasons. Sundials were designed to show twelve hours, following the shadow of the sun. Water clocks, called clepsydra, were used by the Greeks. It was the monk Gerbert who made the first clock around 99 A.D.

3 FRACTIONS

Learning Objective: To introduce fractions in their simplest form.

WHO HAS A WHOLE APPLE?

Equipment. Apples (one for each pair of children); a knife.

Procedure. Ask: What do I have here in my hand? Yes, this is an apple. It is one whole apple. Now I'm cutting it. Hold up half an apple. Ask: Is this a whole apple? No, it is just part of the apple.

Say: Now I put the two parts together again. It is a whole apple. Who wants to take part away? Thank you, Steve. Now what do I have? Yes, I have part of an apple, and Steve has part of an apple.

Give every other child a whole apple, then ask: Who has a whole apple? Who has none? I'm going to cut Jimmy's apple and give some to Debbie. Who has part of an apple? Who else has part of an apple?

Demonstrate *whole* and *part* with each pair of youngsters. When all the children have used the words, let them eat the apples.

To the Teacher. If the activity requires the children to touch, taste, and smell as well as see and hear, the learning experience will have more meaning for them.

DID BOBBY PICK UP ALL THE BLOCKS?

Equipment. Puzzles, blocks, or any group of toys.

Procedure. SAY: You seem to have had a good time playing with the toys today. Have you put everything away yet?

Bobby, you were playing with the blocks. Did you pick up all the blocks? Bobby says he did. Do the rest of you agree? Denise found some more blocks to put in the bag. Now are the blocks all put away?

What does the word *all* mean? Are there any blocks left? No, there aren't any more. Every block that we have is in the bag. There are no blocks left on the floor. All the blocks are picked up.

Here is a puzzle. Pam, you were working with it. Is the puzzle all here? Look at it carefully. What is missing? Are all the pieces here?

To the Teacher. When they are working with a specific group of toys such as trucks or a puzzle, encourage the children to decide if all or only part of them are there. With practice, they will be able to tell the difference between *most, part of,* and *all.* It is more difficult for them to recognize *all* as related to scattered objects—"Are all the windows closed?"—but some children will be able to grasp these ideas as well.

IS THERE ONE FOR PHILIP?

Equipment. Paper (one sheet for each pair of children).

Procedure. ASK: If I have one piece of paper and Philip and Gary both want to color, what can we do? Do you have any ideas?

Philip has suggested that we tear the paper into two parts. Would that work? Let's try it. Do you both have paper to use? Now they each have part of the paper.

Here is one piece of paper, but Joan and Sylvia both need paper. How can they each have some? Could we tear the paper into two parts? Then each of them would have part of it to use.

Demonstrate this activity with each pair of children. The torn edges help to illustrate how the parts can fit back into the original whole.

To the Teacher. Cookies, carrots, boxes of crayons, and many supplies can be divided between the children. Use these opportunities to talk about the terms *whole* and *part.* As they grasp the meanings of these words, they are learning the basis for more complicated fractions.

HOW CAN TWO BOYS EAT ONE BANANA?

Equipment. A banana, cookie, and cupcake; a knife.

Procedure. SAY: Both Allan and Terry want this banana. Is it possible for both of them to eat the same banana? How can two boys eat one banana? Could we divide the banana into two parts? What would we have then? Each boy could have half the banana, couldn't he?

Could we do the same thing with this cookie? Betty, will you break the cookie in two so that you and Tricia can share it? Who has half? Who has the other half?

Will someone cut this cupcake so that two people could share it? What do we have now? Is the cupcake whole? No. There are now two halves to be shared by two people.

To the Teacher. Division of food is an excellent way of demonstrating halves, as the children will be careful to divide equally if they do not know which part they will receive. Use the terms *half* and *whole* as you have the children divide things in half.

HOW MANY PIECES ARE IN THE PUZZLE NOW?

Equipment. A puzzle.

Procedure. Show the children a complete puzzle. SAY: Let's play a game with this puzzle. First, can someone tell me if all the pieces are in the puzzle now? Are all the pieces there? Look closely. Yes, all the pieces are there.

Remove a few pieces, then say: Now I've made some changes. Are all the pieces in the puzzle now? They aren't; you're right! Are most of the pieces in it? Yes, most of them are there. Only a few are gone.

Remove some more pieces. SAY: Now tell me about the pieces in the puzzle. Are they all there? Are most of them there? How many are there? Yes, about half the pieces are in the puzzle.

Robin, take out the rest of the pieces. Now how many pieces are left in this puzzle? Are any of them there? No! None of the pieces are in the puzzle.

To the Teacher. Do not count the pieces in a demonstration such as this one. Counting will confuse the children. Here, only try to help them estimate *half* and *most,* and to recognize *all* and *none.* Have them play the same sort of guessing game with one another.

HOW MANY CRAYONS DO I HAVE NOW?

Equipment. A small box of new crayons.

Procedure. SAY: Here is a new box of crayons. Look inside. Is the box full of crayons? Are the crayons all in the box? Is there room for another crayon: Now watch closely. Remove the crayons, then ask: Are there any crayons in the box? The box is empty, isn't it? How many crayons are there? There are none.

Replace half the crayons, then ask: How many crayons do you see in the box now? Are there none? Are the crayons all there? They are about half there, aren't they?

SAY: Now I'll add a few more. Are the crayons all there? No, there are still spaces for more crayons; you're right. Most of the crayons are in the box now.

To the Teacher. Do not confuse the children by counting or asking them to count the crayons. You want them to estimate when the crayons are *all* there, when there are *none*, when *half* are there, and when *most* of them are there. Reinforce the children's knowledge of these skills at every opportunity by asking them about quantities of crackers, cookies, drinks, and toys.

IS YOUR BOX FINISHED?

Equipment. Puzzles—some finished, some incomplete; a project that requires several days to complete, such as the one described below requiring small boxes, scraps of fabric, glue, and scissors.

Procedure. SAY: Here are some puzzles that you worked on today. Let's play a game with them. I want you to try to tell which puzzles are finished. Here is Chris's puzzle. Is it finished? Why isn't it finished? How can you tell? What does *finished* mean?

Discuss the other puzzles in the same manner. As you discuss whether the puzzles are finished, encourage them to use terms such as *none, some,* and *finished*. Then say: We are going to start a project today that will take us several days to finish. Some of you may finish before others. When you are finished, you can tell us and show us what you've done.

I have a small box for each of you. Today we'll start to make a very pretty and very special box from it. You might want to give your finished box to your mom and dad.

Have the children cut large scraps of fabric into smaller pieces.

Assist them if they need help. Then give them each a box and some glue and have them cover the box with a patchwork of fabric scraps. Remind them that each piece they glue must be held in place for a while. Allow several days for this project. At the end of each work session, compare the boxes. The following day, review which boxes are half done, less than half done, or more than half done. As each child finishes his box, allow him to show it to the others and compare it to boxes in other stages of completion.

To the Teacher. When children create, it is often difficult to recognize whether the art work or construction is finished. One way is to ask, "Do you want to paint any more?" Avoid stating whether the project is finished or not before the child has had a chance to answer.

IS IT ALL GONE?

Equipment. Examples of empty containers—pitcher, cup, box, carton.

Procedure. SAY: Look at this pitcher. There is nothing in it. There was water in it, but Ken poured the water out. The water is all gone.

What is in the cup? Where did the milk go? It is all gone.

Have you finished washing the doll's dishes, Pam? Let's pour the water down the drain now. Is there any water left? It's all gone.

Ralph, would you give me a cracker from the cracker box? Why can't I have a cracker? They are all gone, aren't they? Where did the crackers go? We ate them all, didn't we?

To the Teacher. Preschoolers are often unwilling to accept the fact that something is "all gone" even when they understand it. Help them recognize that when something is all gone there is nothing left. Perhaps more of the same thing can be acquired later, but for now, the crackers or cookies are all gone.

Let them play a guessing game, using a toy and a box. Have them guess "Is it all gone?" and then open the box to see if they guessed correctly.

IS THIS HALF THE PLAYDOUGH?

Equipment. Playdough.

Procedure. SAY: Today you are going to make some things with this playdough. Would you like some now? I'm going to open the can and give half of the playdough to Richard and half of it to Jennifer.

Divide the playdough unevenly, then ask: Did each of you get half of the playdough? How do you know you didn't get half, Jennifer? Yes, Richard's piece is bigger than yours. What does *half* mean? Are pieces cut in half the same size? If you'll both give it back, I'll cut it again. Now did each of you get half?

Let each child have a chance to divide the playdough in half. Let the other children decide if the pieces are equal.

To the Teacher. Cutting the playdough unevenly is a good way to reinforce the idea of halves being equal parts. The children want equal parts and will be quick to call any inequality to your attention. Be sure each child is given the opportunity to divide the playdough in half. They will soon realize that it isn't always easy to divide things equally.

DOES THIS HAND HAVE ALL, OR NONE?

Equipment. A handful of marbles.

Procedure. ASK: Do you see these marbles? They are all in this hand. There are none in the other hand. Now I'll put my hands behind my back. Maybe I moved the marbles. Put one hand in front. ASK: Does this hand have all, or none?

Let the children take turns guessing. The successful guesser can come up and, with help from you, be It.

Let all the children have a turn touching as well as seeing and saying *all* and *none*.

To the Teacher. Sometimes a quiet child hesitates to take his turn. You may give him confidence by standing close by when it is his turn.

ARE WE ALL HERE?

Equipment. Hook, chair, pillow, and other objects for each child.

Procedure. ASK: Are we all here? Al, you are here. Where is your friend Art? Will you all look around for your friends? Is there anyone who isn't here today?

SAY: Now cover your eyes while I have someone hide behind the piano. Can you guess who is missing? (This is a good opportunity to bring attention to a shy child.)

When the missing one has been guessed, repeat the game.

Now have each child choose an object and bring it to you. Explain that the pillow is Al's; the chair is Bevan's, and so on. Have the children place the objects in a pile in the center of the room. SAY: Now turn around and close your eyes. While the children aren't looking, remove several objects and hide them.

SAY: Open your eyes and find your object in the pile. Does everyone have his object? Who doesn't? Are all the things here? How can you tell they aren't? Let the children whose articles are missing go

on a treasure hunt for these things. When they find them, ask: Now, are all the things here?

Repeat the game, taking away and hiding several different objects each time until every child has had the opportunity to look for something.

To the Teacher. These may become favorite games. After all the children understand the rules, try variations of each. In the first one, for example, have two children, or no child, hide.

IS THE BUILDING FINISHED?

Equipment. A construction site to visit; dress-up clothes.

Procedure. ASK: Have you ever watched a road or a building being built? Was it interesting to watch? Who worked on the building? What tools did they use? Would you like to visit a place where a building is being built?

Take the children to a construction site and let them watch the men and equipment working. When you come back to the classroom, talk about whether or not the building was finished.

ASK: How do you know the building isn't finished yet? What is still left to be done? Would you say the building is half done?

The children can play a game called "Are You Finished?" with dress-up clothes. One can put on a hat and gloves and the others can ask, "Are you finished?" The hat- and glove-wearer may decide to add a scarf, or to be finished.

To the Teacher. Children are often told "finish your carrots" when they do not understand what the word means. As you give children opportunities to hear and use new words, you are increasing their ability to learn.

VOCABULARY

Learning Objective: To acquaint the children, through practical experience, with selected mathematical terms.

WHERE IS THE OTHER PART?

Equipment. A broken toy, a repaired toy, a complete puzzle; puzzles for the children to put together, some whole, some with pieces missing.

Procedure. Hold up a broken toy. Ask: What is wrong with this toy truck? Is it broken? Why do you say it's broken? What is missing? Yes, the part with the wheels is missing from the back. Is this toy whole? No, a broken toy is not whole.

Show the children a repaired toy. Say: This baby doll was broken. Do you remember when the head came off? Is it broken now? The head has been fixed. Is the doll whole now? Yes, it is. Even though part was broken, it's all there now.

Point to a complete puzzle. Ask: Is this puzzle all here? Are all the parts in place? Is it broken? No, you're right, it's whole.

Divide the class into groups of two and give each pair a puzzle to put together. Be sure to remove a piece or two from half the puzzles. Say: Some of these puzzles are whole, and some have pieces missing. When you finish working, raise your hand if your puzzle is missing a piece. I have some extra pieces in my pocket. Maybe one of them will fit your puzzle.

To the Teacher. Young children do not always recognize that a whole (puzzle) is made up of parts (pieces). If you hold up a piece from a popular puzzle, some children will recognize it immediately as "part of the farmer puzzle," and others will not even identify it as part of a puzzle.

HOW BIG IS IT?

Equipment. Toys that range from small to large.

Procedure. SAY: Here is a big pile of toys that I've found in our room. Let's play a game with them. We can divide these toys into two piles. We'll put the small ones over here and the large ones over here.

SAY: Each of you pick up a toy and decide if it is small or large. Then put the toy in the right pile. Keep putting the toys in these piles until they are all gone.

Discuss the children's placement of the toys when they are done. Ask questions such as: Does this stuffed animal belong here in the small pile? Where would a real lion belong? Is this box large or small?

To the Teacher. Children tend to exaggerate, so listen carefully to their descriptions of things. Have them compare the large and small objects by placing them beside each other. The terms may become confusing if you use too large a scale of comparison. For example, the table may be large compared to the crayon box, but small compared to the building itself. Use objects of obvious but moderate difference in size.

WHICH IS LARGEST?

Equipment. A coat hanger bent into a circle; a table with groups of objects ranging from small to large, no more than five objects to a group.

Procedure. SAY: I have placed lots of things on our long table today. We're going to play a game with them. To play this game you must know what the words *smallest* and *biggest* mean. Hold up your hand, then ask: Which finger is smallest? Which finger is biggest?

ASK: Who would like to go first? Wesley, take this circle I've made from a coat hanger and put it over the largest object in this group. Good. Now can you put it over the smallest object?

Allow each child to use the circle to identify smallest and largest objects in a selected group.

To the Teacher. The children have already compared smaller and bigger. Now they are challenged to look at a larger group of items and choose the smallest and the biggest. Some may have difficulty. Encourage them to pick up the items and hold them side by side to help in their comparison.

HOW MUCH WATER IS THERE?

Equipment. Pitcher of water; containers of various sizes; pan to collect the overflow.

Procedure. After snack one day, say: Now that we've eaten, I want to put away the pitcher. There is still some water left in it.

Will you help me? Here is a cup I can pour the water into. Do you think there is too much water to pour into this cup? Let's see.

Pour the water into containers of various sizes, asking each time if there is too much or too little for the container being filled.

Ask: What does *too much* mean? If there is too much, does the cup run over? Is there still some left that won't fit in the cup?

What does *too little* mean? If there is too little room for this water, will the cup be full? Will there be room for more in the cup?

To the Teacher. Let all the children pour water into small and large containers. If you know that some water will be spilled, you can set up the activity where water will do the least damage.

IS IT TOO HEAVY TO LIFT?

Equipment. Objects of approximately equal size, some heavy, some light, such as a hollow block, book, empty box, full box.

Procedure. Ask: Has your mom ever told you that you were getting too heavy to lift? What does that mean? What does something heavy feel like? Is it easy to lift? Is it hard to lift? If something is too heavy, can you lift it?

Say: Let's look at these things and decide if they are heavy or light. Some of them you may have lifted before. Can you remember if the block is heavy or light? Sandy, will you lift the block? Is it easy to lift? Is it light or heavy?

Jeanie, will you pick up this book? Is it easy to lift? Is it hard to lift? Is the book heavy or light?

Play "Heavy or Light" in the following manner. Show the children identical boxes, one empty, one containing a heavy object. Ask: Which one is heavy, Wendy? Beth, pick up the boxes and see if Wendy was right.

Now move the boxes and let someone else guess.

To the Teacher. The children will enjoy discovering which things are heavy and which are light. They may be amazed that they can pick up things that are large but light. They may realize that two people can pick up a heavy object when one cannot. An object that is heavy to one child may not seem heavy to another. As the children go about their daily activities, ask them occasionally if that doll or that truck is heavy, or light. Give them many opportunities to use these terms.

WHICH PICTURE COMES FIRST?

Equipment. Pictures of children and adults of all ages, sequences of three simple pictures that tell a story.

Procedure. SAY: Let's sit down in a circle and look at some pictures. Note which child sits down first, then ask: Jerome, did you sit down before or after Leroy? Did you sit down first? You sat down before Leroy, then, didn't you? Tina, did you sit down before or after Andy? Did you sit down last? Is that *before* or *after?*

Hold up several pictures, including one of a baby. SAY: Here are some pictures of people. Which picture comes first? Was the person a baby first? This picture should come before the others then. Which picture comes next? What about this one of the boy on his bike? Does it come after the baby? Here is a picture of a daddy. Where should it come? Which picture is before this one? Which one is after?

These pictures tell a story. Can you tell what happened first? What happened next? What happened after that?

To the Teacher. The children have had experiences of being first and last or before and after others. Now they are using this concept to relate to ideas and their proper order. Help them place pictures and ideas in sequence, using the terms *before* and *after*.

WHAT IS A CIRCLE?

Equipment. Jar lids, bottle caps, toys with wheels, blocks (both round and other shapes).

Procedure. Hold up a wheel. SAY: Can everybody see this round wheel? How does it move? Tony, can you spin the wheel? It is round.

Trace your finger around the edge of the wheel, then draw a circle in the air. SAY: This is a circle. Can you make your arm go around and draw a circle?

Point to the jar lids. Ask: What shape are these lids? Are the bottle caps the same shape? Give each child a circular object and have him trace his finger around it. Have the children name other round shapes they see.

Point to the blocks and ask: Can you find the blocks that have this same round shape? Show me how you can trace around the circle with your finger.

Then say: Now let's all make a circle! Let's stand up and join hands. Who would like to run around the outside of our circle? Who wants to stand inside our circle?

To the Teacher. It takes time for children to learn the difference between a circle and a round object. Some children realize that wheels "work" because they are round. If you provide construction toys for building cars or wagons, the children will soon observe the advantage of the wheel.

You might want to serve round cookies from a round plate after you try this activity.

WHAT IS A TRIANGLE?

Equipment. A musical triangle, triangular blocks, felt triangles, squares, and circles; a flannelboard.

Procedure. Tap the triangle, then ask: Did you hear that sound? Who would like to tap the triangle? As the children take turns holding the instrument, let them trace around the shape with a finger.

After everyone has had a turn, say: Let's each draw a big triangle in the air. Look at this triangle as you draw. Make your finger go across, and up, and back down.

Hold up a felt triangle. Say: This is a triangle, too. Now I'm going to put it on the flannelboard. Who can find another triangle to put beside it? Hold up a square, then a circle. Each time, ask: Is this a triangle? Have the children pick out all the felt triangles and put them on the flannelboard.

To the Teacher. The children will need to review these shapes many times. Actually feeling the outlines of shapes helps many to learn.

You might plan to serve triangular crackers for snack the day you introduce this shape.

WHAT IS A SQUARE?

Equipment. Square blocks, drinking straws, construction sticks or pencils; square objects placed around the room, one for each child to find.

Procedure. Hold up a square block. ASK: Is this square block a circle? No, it isn't round, is it? We call it a square. See how straight the sides are? What other things are square like this?

Pick up other objects in the room and ask each time: Is it a square?

Make a square using four drinking straws, construction toys, sticks, or pencils, then ask: Would someone else like to make a square? Give the child exactly four sticks to work with.

SAY : Let's have a treasure hunt now. All over the room I've hidden square things. Look until you find something square. When you have found one, come to our circle and sit down. Then we'll share the square things you've found.

To the Teacher. Young children often will label a rectangle as a square. They will often say, for example, that a book or a box is square when it is actually rectangular. It is not important to tell them the difference, since they cannot measure. If a child brings back an object that isn't square, be careful not to criticize. Rather, encourage him to hunt again for a square.

At snack time, you might want to serve square crackers on square placemats.

I'M THINKING OF A SHAPE.

Equipment. A mental or actual list of objects in the room that are shaped like squares, circles, or triangles.

Procedure. SAY: Today we're going to play a guessing game with shapes. I wonder how good you are at guessing. I'm going to think of an object in our room. I'll describe it to you. If you think you know what I'm describing, you raise your hand and tell us your guess. Ready?

I'm thinking of an object. It is shaped like a triangle. It is green. Can you guess what I'm thinking of? (A green block.)

I'm thinking of another object in our room. It is shaped like a circle. It is white and there are blue flowers on it. What am I thinking of? (A play dish from the kitchen area.)

I'm thinking of an object that is square. It is bright red and very big. You'll need to look on the walls to find this shape. What am I thinking of? (The bulletin board.)

Continue in this manner as long as the children appear interested. Later, they may want to take turns thinking of a shape and describing it to the others.

To the Teacher. This activity will provide a good review of shapes the children have been exposed to. Be sure the objects you think of and describe are in plain view of the children, and praise them for their responses. If a child hesitates to join in, ask her to look around the room for a certain shape.

When the guessing game is over, ask all the children to find examples of certain shapes, assigning, for example, a square to Bobby, a triangle to Michele, and so on. If they know their colors, you might specify an orange rectangle or a purple circle.

ARE THE BIRDS STANDING ON CIRCLES?

Equipment. Cut large shapes from contact paper in four different colors—two red squares, three green triangles, four blue circles, and five black stars (or one shape of each color for each child). Attach these to the floor in groups by shape—the two squares together, and so on.

Procedure. ASK: Do you notice anything different on the floor today? What are they? Who can tell me what these are? How many squares are there? Continue to ask similar questions until the children have identified all the shapes, numbers, and colors.

Divide the class into four groups. Give each group a name—Birds, Dogs, Cats, Lions. Ask the Lions to stand on the squares, the Dogs on the circles, the Cats on the triangles, the Birds on the stars.

Continue with the game, telling the teams where to stand, changing your directions each time. For example, one time mention the shape, another time the color, and a third time the number involved.

Repeat the game if the children enjoy it and allow them to call out directions after they see how it's played. You might assign each group a leader. The team leader could say, "Now we'll go to the squares." The leader of the squares would then name a place for that team to go.

To the Teacher. This activity offers an excellent review of colors, shapes, and numbers. It should be used as a review just for fun after the children are thoroughly acquainted with these concepts. Keep this game fast-moving.

ARE THESE SHOES THE SAME?

Equipment. Items that don't match—mittens, socks, boots, shoes; drawing on chalkboard of three faces, two of which are the same.

Procedure. AsK: When it's cold outside, what do we wear on our hands? We need mittens, don't we? Here are some mittens, lots of mittens! Donna, can you find two mittens that are the same? Are these mittens that Donna chose the same? Why don't these two mittens match? One is blue and one is brown; that's right. We need to find a blue one or a brown one to have two mittens the same. Erik, can you find a mitten that is different from this one? It doesn't match, does it?

Let the children choose items from other groups (socks, shoes, boots, and so on) that are the same. Talk about how the items are different.

Then point to the chalkboard. SAY: Here is a drawing of three faces. Can you find the two faces that are the same? These two happy faces are the same. Why is this face different? You're right. This face is crying.

To the Teacher. As you choose items for the children to match, be careful to use obvious matches rather than difficult ones. The children need to experience success quickly as they look for items that are the same. It may be more difficult for them to recognize pictures that are the same than those that are different.

WHO HAS MORE?

Equipment. Two glasses and a pitcher of water; two containers, sand or flour to fill the containers.

Procedure. SAY: I'm going to pour both Lisa and Vickie a drink. Can you tell me whose cup has more water in it? You say Lisa's cup has more. How can you tell there is more in this cup? Is the cup fuller? Can you see more in it? Does Vickie's cup have less?

SAY: Let's pour sand into both these jars. Which jar has less sand? How can you tell there is less? Is the other jar fuller than this one?

ASK: What does *more* mean? Can you tell by looking that there is more? If this jar is full, is there more, or less in it than this jar that is empty?

To the Teacher. Children notice when someone has more to drink or a larger share of anything. Help them with the vocabulary. Introduce the term *less* and try to use it as often as you use *more*. The children are not as familiar with that word. Avoid counting objects as you help them understand these terms.

WHO'S BOTH?

Equipment. Crayons, blocks, or other objects in groups of two.

Procedure. SAY: If I ask both Jerry and Ron to stand by the door, what would you boys do? Show me. What does the word *both* mean? Do two of you have to stand by the door if both of you are there? Does *both* mean two?

Sonja, here are two crayons. Will you put both crayons on the table? What will Sonja do now? Will she put one, or two crayons on the table? Does *both* mean two?

I want each person here to stand up. Everyone stood up! What does *each* mean? Will each person who has on a blue shirt sit down? Does *each* mean one? Can it mean more than one?

ASK: Will you each put a pencil in this box? How many pencils did you put in the box? Can *each* mean one?

To the Teacher. The children may use these terms in a routine way, but they may not be able to define either one. *Both* is easier to comprehend as it always means two. *Each* means all of a said thing, but is confusing because the number may change. For this term, the children must note what the object is and perform the given function for all the objects involved.

CAN WE HAVE MORE COOKIES?

Equipment. A cookie plate with only a few cookies; empty boxes; a variety of containers and small objects, such as marbles, crayons, and others; a box full of cotton.

Procedure. SAY: Look at this cookie plate. Are there lots of cookies on it? Are there enough cookies for everyone to have one? Why not? Are there more children than cookies? When these are gone, will there be any left? Will the plate be empty?

ASK: What does *empty* mean? Is this room empty? Why not? Is my purse empty? Is this cereal box empty? How can you tell? Is there any cereal in it?

Here are some other containers. Look at each one carefully. Can you find an empty container? Shirley has found one. Shirley, can you make the container *not* empty? How would you do that?

Allow the children time to play with the containers and small objects, filling and emptying them. Ask each child to show you an empty container. For added fun, pass around a box full of cotton. Ask the children to shake it and feel it, but not to open it. Then ask if they think it is empty. They will probably be surprised to learn it is full!

To the Teacher. Through this activity, the children learn the meaning of *empty* by comparing empty containers to those that contain something. Emphasize that *empty* means *none*, as opposed to *some*, *a few*, or *full*. Preschool children are usually familiar with the word *full*. It is easy for them to see when a container will hold no more. The word *empty*, however, is not used as often and will need more explanation. Ask the children often if this or that is empty: Is the sink empty? Is your cup empty? Be sure to ask why it is or isn't empty.

WILL IT GO FAST?

Equipment. Ramp from chair or table to floor; things to slide down or push up the ramp—truck, car, block, paper wad, ball, pencil.

Procedure. ASK: Who would like to race for us today? When I say "Go," Lee and Barbara will run from here to the table. When the race is over, ask: Who ran fast? Both of them are fast runners, aren't they? Who got there first? Is it fun to run fast?

SAY: Let's use this board to make a ramp from the table down to the floor. Let's see if this truck will go fast or slowly down the ramp. Was that one fast? Did it go down the ramp in a hurry? Is that fast?

Now try this paper wad on the ramp. Does it go down in a hurry? Is it fast? It moves slowly, doesn't it? It takes a long time for the paper to get to the bottom. We even have to help it a little.

Let's try some other things on the ramp. I'll let you decide if they are fast or slow.

To the Teacher. This might be a good time to tell the story of the tortoise and the hare. Talk about animals that move fast and those that are slow, such as a snail and a bird, or a squirrel and an ant. Have the children try pushing the objects up the ramp. Ask each time whether they go fast or slow.

WHERE DO WE PLAY BASEBALL?

Equipment. Pictures of outdoor and indoor activities and scenes; a shoe box, some dolls.

Procedure. ASK: Are we inside or outside right now? How do you know we're inside? Is there a roof above us and walls around us? Can we feel the breeze or the rain while we're inside?

How is it different outside? Is there a roof? Are there walls? Can you feel the snow or wind or sunshine outside?

SAY: Here are some pictures of people doing things. Let's play a guessing game with the pictures. Where do you play with a ball and bat? Why do you play outside? What would happen if you played a ball game inside?

Here is another picture. Do you like to watch television? Where do you watch it, inside or outside? Why do we usually watch TV inside? What could happen to the TV if we put it outside?

Put the dolls in the shoe box, then say: Let's pretend this shoe box is a house. Where are the dolls now? How do you know they are inside? Are there walls and a roof?

To the Teacher. The children should have little difficulty distinguishing between inside and outside. Have them talk about what they find and do outdoors versus indoors. Use small objects to reinforce their understanding of *inside* and *outside* by having them place things inside and outside a box.

WHAT'S INSIDE THE BALL?

Equipment. Two chocolate bunnies, one hollow and one solid; solid and hollow balls; a knife.

Procedure. ASK: Do you like candy? I can imagine that all of you do! Have you ever seen chocolate bunnies like these? Have you ever eaten one? What did you find inside the bunny? SAY: Let's cut this candy with a knife. What's inside? Is there more chocolate? Are there any holes? This candy is solid. There are no holes inside, just more candy when we cut it.

Pick up the hollow bunny. SAY: Now let's cut this candy. What's inside? Is there more chocolate? There isn't, is there? What do you see? There's a hole inside! This candy is hollow. It's empty. There's no more chocolate. Now that it is cut up, let's eat it.

Show the children two balls. SAY: Here are two balls. Can you find out which one is solid and which is hollow? This ball comes apart. Is there anything inside? Is this ball hollow? What about this rubber ball? Does it come apart? How can you tell what's inside? When you squeeze it, does it feel solid or hollow?

To the Teacher. ·Both the terms *solid* and *hollow* will be unfamiliar to the children. They are not used often, so find as many examples as possible to reinforce their understanding of the terms. Ask them to guess about those objects that can't be cut open and to shake, squeeze, and lift the objects for clues.

ARE THERE ENOUGH NAPKINS?

Equipment. Items for each child, such as cups, napkins, crayons.

Procedure. SAY: It's time to set our tables for snack. Are there enough paper napkins in this pile for everyone to have one? How can we be sure? If everyone takes a napkin, can we tell?

Allow everyone to help himself, then ask: Did everyone get a napkin? Were there enough? How do you know? What does *enough* mean? Are there as many napkins as we need?

When it's time for an art activity, ask: Will you give everyone a crayon, Willy? Were there enough crayons? Since Willy didn't have one for himself, were there enough? No! We need one more. Here's one. Now are there enough? Are there as many crayons as we need?

ASK: Are there enough trucks in this room for everyone to play with one at the same time? No, there aren't enough trucks to go around, are there? Are there enough toys in the room for everyone to have one to play with? Yes, there are as many toys as there are people.

To the Teacher. The term *enough* is closely related to the term *as many as*. Avoid having the children count objects or counting for them. Help them, rather, to comprehend that if there are as many as needed, then there are enough.

IS MY HAIR LONGER THAN TAMMY'S?

Equipment. Objects of various lengths.

Procedure. Ask: Is Tammy's hair longer or shorter than my hair? How can you tell? Does Tammy's hair come down to her shoulders? Does mine?

Try playing a game using *longer* and *shorter*. Begin by naming a medium-sized object in the room, such as a chair. Ask a child to name something in the room that is longer than the chair. Ask another child to name something shorter.

After the children are well acquainted with these terms, add the words *taller*, *bigger*, and *smaller*.

To the Teacher. The terms longer and shorter are closely related to taller, larger, and smaller. Be sure the children know the differences between these words.

5 COUNTING

Learning Objective: To introduce, through games and rhymes, the numbers 1 to 6.

DO YOU HAVE THREE FEET?

Equipment. None.

Procedure. SAY: Let's play a silly game. You tell me if I'm right or wrong in what I say. You have three feet! (Let the children count their own feet to check.) You have four eyes! (Let them touch their own to be sure.) You have two mouths! You have five ears! You have one hand! You have three legs!

After everyone has a good laugh, repeat the silly lines. Have the children check on themselves and answer, "We have two feet, we have two eyes," and so forth.

To the Teacher. Young children delight in silly games and will love the thought of themselves or others with five ears or three feet. Capitalize on their sense of humor as you help them recognize the two's on their own bodies.

HOW MANY STARS DO YOU HAVE?

Equipment. Gummed stars and paper; two stars on a chart or paper, other groups of two.

Procedure. Put two stars on a piece of paper, then ask: Can someone count the stars for us? How many stars are on this paper? There are two stars, aren't there? Will you make a picture like this one for your very own? Here are some stars to lick and stick on. Be sure that you count out two stars.

To the Teacher. The children may enjoy licking the gummed stars and take extra ones. Be sure that they understand the quantity. Watch carefully as each chooses his two stars.

ONE, TWO, BUCKLE MY SHOE.

Equipment. None.

Procedure. SAY: Let's have some fun counting today. We'll use a rhyme to help us. Some of you have said this rhyme before. Now let's say it together. As we say the numbers, let's hold up the fingers for each one.

One, two	*Pick up sticks;*
Buckle my shoe;	*Seven, eight,*
Three, four,	*Lay them straight;*
Knock at the door;	*Nine, ten,*
Five, six,	*A good, fat hen.*

To the Teacher. It is essential that the children know the words to the counting rhymes before they can show the numbers with their fingers. Take time to teach the rhymes thoroughly first. You'll find additional rhymes on later pages.

Use these as a relaxing, enjoyable way to practice counting. Look for songs that use numbers, too. When possible, make up or use suggested motions to the rhymes and songs. The gestures, such as holding up two fingers for the numeral two, reinforce the words.

HOW MANY TRICYCLES DO WE HAVE?

Equipment. Three tricycles or pictures of three tricycles; a picture of three children; other objects grouped in threes.

Procedure. SAY: Here are pictures of some tricycles. We need to decide if there are enough tricycles for Janie, Tony, and Freddy to ride. How can we tell?

Let's count the tricycles. Count with me: One, two, three. How many tricycles are there? How many children are there? Are there enough tricycles for each child to ride one? Yes, there are three children and three tricycles.

SAY: I put some pencils in this box. Can you tell me how many there are? Hold up a finger for each pencil. How many fingers and how many pencils do you count? Could Janie, Tony, and Freddy each have one?

To the Teacher. Try these counting rhymes:

> *1, 2,*
> *I like you.*
>
> *1, 2, 3,*
> *Mother loves me.*
>
> *1, 2, 3, 4,*
> *There are no more.*
>
> *1, 2, 3, 4, 5!*
> *I caught a cat alive;*
> *6, 7 8, 9, 10!*
> *I let it go again.*
>
> *1, 2, 3, 4, 5, 6,*
> *Let me see you do some tricks!*

HOW MANY WHEELS CAN YOU COUNT?

Equipment. A bicycle, tricycle, and wagon (or illustrations of these).

Procedure. SAY: Here are some toys you can ride. They all have wheels. How many wheels does the bicycle have? Count them with me: one, two. Can you show me two fingers?

How many wheels does the tricycle have? Let's count them together: one, two, three. Can you hold up three fingers?

How many wheels does the wagon have? Can you count them? Show me four fingers. How many wheels are in the front? How many are in the back? How many are there in all?

Now let's look for some other things on these toys. How many pedals are on the tricycle? How many are on the bicycle? Do both toys have two pedals? How many seats does each one have?

To the Teacher. It's helpful to use objects the children can touch. Whenever possible, give them a chance to touch as they count. Showing the number with their fingers is a good means of reinforcement.

WHICH PILE HAS THREE?

Equipment. Groups of crayons, buttons, toys, and blocks in two's, three's, and four's; pictures on the chalkboard or bulletin board of the same groupings.

Procedure. ASK: Can anyone count to three? Most of you can! Let's count to three together: one, two, three. Can you hold up three fingers? Good. Now let's look for groups of three things.

Arrange the objects in groups of two's, three's, and four's on a table. Make sure there is a group of three for each child. ASK: Now can each of you find a group of three things? When you've found three things that are the same, take them and sit on the floor.

SAY: Now all of you have something to share. Let's look at what you found and count together to see if there are three. How many crayons does Louise have? Let's count them together.

After you follow this procedure with each child, say: There are some pictures on the chalkboard. Can someone tell us which pictures have three's in them? Are there three faces? Are there three boxes?

To the Teacher. It is important that the children recognize the group of three before they attempt to compare three to the other groups. At first, you'll need to work with groups of three only. Then by using comparison, encourage the children to find groups of three mixed in with other groups. Introduce the term *as many as* and have the children show, by comparison, that there are as many crayons as there are pencils, buttons, and so on.

HOW OLD ARE YOU?

Equipment. None.

Procedure. Ask: Do you know how old you are? Who can tell me? Do you know how many fingers that is?

Some children can perform this task quite well. For them, the lesson could be directed to comparison and contrast. Ask: Who else is holding up four fingers? Who isn't? How many do you have, Virginia?

Some children have never held up fingers to represent their age. To teach this to a child, hold your hand in the appropriate position and let him imitate you. Then count his age, first on your hand, then on his.

It requires considerable coordination for young children to hold up three fingers, for example, so praise the children as they experience success.

To the Teacher. Here's another counting rhyme:

> *One—two—three*
> *Mother—Daddy—me.*

Have the children point to each finger in turn as they say the rhyme.

HOW MANY FEET DOES AN ELEPHANT HAVE?

Equipment. Pictures of animals with four feet.

Procedure. Ask: How many feet have you? Ann, will you count yours for us? Who wants to be an elephant? When a child is on all fours, count his feet. Ask: Does the elephant have the same number of feet Ann does?

Say: Look at this picture of the dog. How many feet does the dog have? It has four, doesn't it? Is the dog like the elephant?

Can you think of other animals that have four feet? Everybody choose a partner. One of you can pretend he is a dog. The other can count the dog's feet.

Have the children count aloud—one, two, three, four—and touch the dog's feet as they count.

To the Teacher. A four-footed classroom pet (hamster, gerbil, or rabbit) gives the children an opportunity to observe how the four feet are vital to the animal's balance.

HOW MANY WINDOWS DO YOU SEE?

Equipment. A picture of a house with five windows; paper and crayons for each child.

Procedure. Ask: Who can count to five? Good. Now let's count together. Will you show me five fingers on one hand? Hold up two fingers, then ask: Is this five?

Show the children the picture of the house. Ask: How many windows do you see in this house. Let's count: one, two, three, four, five. There are five windows in the house.

Say: I've got a piece of paper and some crayons for everyone. I want each of you to draw a picture of five toys. Draw any kind of toy you like, but be sure there are five.

To the Teacher. You might want to introduce this rhyme:

This is one,
This is two.
This is my hand,
And this is my shoe.

Let the children imitate you as you demonstrate:

One finger,
Two fingers.
One hand,
One foot.

WHICH HANDS MATCH?

Equipment. Five cards—on one is a hand with one finger extended, on the others are illustrations of hands with two, three, four, and five fingers extended; five piles of toys illustrating the numbers one through five.

Procedure. SAY: Here are some cards to use in a matching game. This card shows one finger. I can make my hand show one finger like this. Are they the same? On this card, how many fingers do you see? Is it like my hand?

Demonstrate this with all five cards, then say: Here are some toys. Can you count the toys? How many are there in this pile? Joyce, can you find the card with three fingers? Do these match? How many fingers are there? How many toys? Yes, there are three toys and three fingers.

ASK: How many balls do you see here? Can you find the card that matches this one? Follow this procedure with each card.

To the Teacher. If a child has difficulty with this exercise, draw around his hand with a crayon to illustrate the shape in each position.

HOW MANY LEGS DO YOU HAVE?

Equipment. Tables, chairs; paper and crayons for each child.

Procedure. SAY: I have four legs! Is that right? It isn't? How many legs do I have? How do you know I have two legs? Can you count them? Count your legs.

There is something in our room today with four legs. Can you find it?

Eric has found something with four legs. Show us, Eric. This table has four legs, doesn't it? Can you count them? People and animals and tables all have legs!

ASK: Can you find anything else in our room with four legs? Does this chair have four legs? Let's count them.

Here is a piece of paper for each of you to draw four legs. Draw a chair or table. Be sure to count the legs.

To the Teacher. The children may not be familiar with the term legs as applied to tables or chairs. To demonstrate the need for four legs to balance a table, build one from blocks with legs in only three of the corners.

CAN YOU SHOW ME HOW MANY WITH YOUR FINGERS?

Equipment. None.

Procedure. SAY: We're going to play a counting game with our fingers and things in our room. When I name something, you show me with your fingers how many of those things there are in our room.

First, look for doors. How many fingers do you need? There is just one door, so you put up one finger.

How many sinks are there? Did you hold up two fingers?

Count the lights and hold up that many fingers. There are three lights.

How many windows do we have? Did you hold up four fingers?

How many tables are there? There are five tables, aren't there?

Can you count the pictures on this bulletin board? How do you show four with your fingers? That's right!

How many dolls are on the shelf? There are two, aren't there? How can you show two with your fingers?

To the Teacher. Some children have difficulty holding up fingers. It requires great coordination to position the fingers in a certain way. Don't ignore problems they may encounter. Instead, stop the activity and talk about why it's hard to use our fingers in certain ways. Practice together the easiest ways to show the numbers one through five with fingers.

WHO HAS THREE CRAYONS?

Equipment. Enough crayons for each child to have not more than five; be sure some children have exactly three crayons.

Procedure. SAY: Here is a big box of crayons. Will each of you come and get some? Now let's talk about your crayons. Will you each count your crayons?

ASK: Who has three crayons? If you have three crayons, come to me. Let's count your crayons together. Now each of you can tell us how many crayons you have.

Carmen, how many do you have? Two, that's right. Would you like to have three crayons? What do you need to do? Yes, get one more. Billy, you have four crayons. Is that more than three? Do you want to put some back so you have only three? Then do that.

Can you all be sure you have just three crayons? If you need more, get them. If you need less, put some back. Now let's count together: one, two, three.

To the Teacher. In addition to recognizing groups of three, the children are challenged here to compare the quantity three to other quantities. It involves adding to or subtracting from their own group of crayons to make three. Do not discuss addition and subtraction as such.

WHO CAN COUNT TO FIVE?

Equipment. Five blocks, five marbles, five crayons, and five each of other objects.

Procedure. Hold up one block and ask: How many blocks are there, Craig? Add another block and ask: How many, Leo? Continue with the marbles, crayons, and other toys, letting all the children answer.

Then say: Who would like to take all five blocks and count them for us? Who can count the crayons?

Can you make a line of five children? Wally, you be in this line. SAY: That's *one*. Who would like to be *two? Three? Four? Five?* Is your line finished? Will you people count yourselves for us?

Who else would like to make a line of five? Give all the children a chance to play.

To the Teacher. The children may ask to repeat some counting activities again and again. Even though they can count to five, they enjoy the repetition. If they liked this game, they could probably do a similar activity with two, three, and four, needing less help from you. Use the same procedure as in the above game, only encourage the children to count and line up: one, two; one, two, three; one, two, three, four.

HOW MANY ARE TWINS?

Equipment. Pictures of twins and other pairs of identical objects.

Procedure. ASK: Do you know any twins? What are twins? Could they be brothers or sisters? How many are twins? Can there be more than two if we call people twins? Twins are always two, aren't they?

SAY: Here are some pictures of twins. Let's count how many are in each picture. Are there two in each picture?

Can you find the twin trucks in this group of trucks? Are there any trucks that are exactly alike? How many are there? Could we call these two trucks twins? If there were three trucks alike, would they be twins? No, because twins are only two.

Did you know that twin babies are born on the same day? Instead of one baby, two are born. These two babies are called twins.

To the Teacher. The children are already familiar with the quantity two. They extend the idea when they learn that twins can only mean two. Say *two* with each picture or example of twins they see.

Some children may have seen twins or may want to tell about twins they know.

WHAT COMES IN PAIRS?

Equipment. Pairs of shoes, boots, socks, mittens; pictures or examples of other things that come in pairs.

Procedure. SAY: Many of you wore boots today because of the snow (or rain) outside. Here is Chuck's boot. Is this one boot all you have, Chuck? Why not? Why do you need two boots? What are these two boots called? What is a *pair*? Are there always two things in a pair? Can you think of other things that come in pairs?

Hold up a pair of socks. SAY: Here are some things you use. What are these things for? Discuss each of the pairs in this manner, then ask: How many socks do you wear at one time? How many shoes? These are called a pair. Are there always two in a pair? Can there be more than two? Can there be less than two? A pair always means two, doesn't it?

Encourage the children to name things that come in pairs. Show and discuss the pictures or examples of pairs that you have prepared. In each case, have a child count how many things are in the pair—two mittens, two socks, two shoes, and so on.

To the Teacher. Some children may be confused by the vocabulary. If they mention twins, emphasize that twins are two people or things that look the same, and pairs refer to objects or items that would be incomplete if there were only one. If they mention pair of pants or pair of scissors, demonstrate the two parts of each. Often a large pair of scissors can be separated by simply removing the screw.

The word *pair* may be confusing to the children, especially to those who like to eat pears! For fun, bring in two pears and talk about a pair of pears. The goal is to develop the concept that a pair contains two like objects.

HOW MANY COOKIES DO WE NEED?

Equipment. Cookies or another treat for the children.

Procedure. Say: Today we are going to have a special treat for you. Do you like cookies? How will I know how many we need? I want to be sure everyone gets one.

Ask: Could we count to learn how many I should bring? Let's count together so we are sure we get the right number.

Count slowly and distinctly as you touch each child's head. Then count these same numbers again as you write them on the chalkboard.

How many children are there in this class? How many cookies do we need?

To the Teacher. The counting by young children is often rote and without an understanding of the meaning of the numbers. Help them count the number of people in class even if they have never counted some of these numbers before. Be sure they have many opportunities to repeat this counting while they can see the objects being counted.

HOW MANY PEOPLE ARE THERE IN YOUR FAMILY?

Equipment. Large piece of paper of each child; crayons.

Procedure. ASK: How many are there in your family, Gerald? As he tells you, draw a circle to represent a head for each one. SAY: Now let's count Nina's family. Nina, will you finish the picture? Now whose family shall we count?

Follow the same procedure with each child. They can complete their pictures by adding eyes, arms, or whatever pleases them.

These pictures may prove interesting to the other children and the families. Display them, asking: Do you remember Kathy's brother who came here one day? This is Gene's baby sister, the one he told us about.

To the Teacher. While the children are drawing, talk to each child about his family. ASK: Can you count the people in your family? Tell me about your picture. Who is each circle for? How many circles do you have? How many are in your family? Do you want me to put their names under their pictures? Some children will need to be reminded of family members they did not include. As they talk about the family group, you will also learn how the child feels about himself.

Some children will want to include grandparents, other relatives, and pets. If they picture more people than they can count, you can count aloud for them.

HOW MUCH MONEY IS IT?

Equipment. Play money—pennies and nickels for each child.

Procedure. ASK: Do you have a bank at home? Why do you have a bank? Do you like to keep money? Who gives you money to put in it? Have you ever earned money?

SAY: Here are two pieces of money—a nickel, and a penny. Do you know which one can buy more? If you guess the bigger one can buy more, you are right. Do you know how much this nickel is worth? One nickel is worth five pennies.

I'm going to give you each a pile of money, and then we'll play a game with it. First, pick out the smallest coin. What is it called?

How many pennies does it take to make a nickel? What is the smallest coin called? What is the largest coin called?

Have the children do other things with the coins such as put all the nickels in a pile, or put all the pennies together. Repeat these activities until the children grasp the differences in appearance. Eventually they will recognize the differences in value as well.

To the Teacher. Some of the children may receive a small allowance or even earn money on occasion. Encourage them to learn the differences in the coins they have. If there is a store nearby where the children could buy things for pennies, you might arrange a shopping trip.

DO THESE MATCH?

Equipment. From several decks of old playing cards, pick out the cards two through six. Use only spades, as they are largest and easiest to see.

Procedure. Ask: Do you like to play cards? Do you have cards like these at home? Let's look at each of these cards and see how many of these black things there are on each one.

Start with two and have them count the two spades. Some may recognize the numeral 2 as well. Have the children study each card with your help so that they understand how to count each one.

Say: Let's play a game with cards like these. Who would like to pick a card? Christin, will you place it on the floor so everyone can see it? Now, who can find a card in this pile that is the same as the one Christin picked? How many black things are on Christin's card? Does this card match? Is it the same? Count the spots.

Continue in this manner, letting one child pick a card and another find a matching one. Each time, talk about the number involved.

To the Teacher. Many children are exposed to cards at home and are fascinated with them. Playing cards can be an excellent teaching aid. Using smaller groups, you could give each child three cards and have them each put one down at a time face up. They must decide whose card is highest, and that person takes all the cards. The person who has the most cards when all are played is the winner.

HOW MANY CLOTHESPINS ARE THERE?

Equipment. A coat hanger and at least six clip-on clothespins.

Procedure. Hold up the coat hanger. ASK: Have you ever seen one of these before? What is it? What are hangers usually used for? We're going to use this hanger for a counting game. I have some clothespins here, too, that we'll use in our game.

SAY: Monica, will you put three clothespins on the hanger? Let's count them. Are there three? Jennifer, I've decided I only want one clothespin on the hanger. Can you change it so there is only one?

Continue the game in this manner, giving each child a chance to add or remove clothespins to make a given number. Include all the numbers one through six.

Have the children take turns asking for certain numbers and designating a person to place the clothespins on the hanger. Be sure everyone has a chance to both give directions and arrange the clothespins.

To the Teacher. After the children have worked with each number individually, one through six, they are ready for this type of review activity. In actuality, they are using simple addition and subtraction to play the game, but you need not be concerned that

they understand that two and two make four. Rather, you want them to be able to recognize a specific number of objects and be able to count that many on the hanger.

ARE THERE AS MANY HOUSES AS TREES?

Equipment. Flannelboard; flannel cut-outs in groups of two, three, four, five, and six, such as two houses, three trees, four faces, five hats, and six sticks.

Procedure. SAY: We're going to use our flannelboard today for a game. I'm going to put some things on it and you are to decide if there are as many of one thing as there are of another.

Place two houses and two trees on the flannelboard. ASK: Are there as many houses as there are trees? How can you tell? Scott, can you make a line with your finger from each house to each tree? Are there as many trees as houses? How many houses are there? How many trees?

Place two houses and three faces on the flannelboard. ASK: Are there as many faces as there are houses? How can you tell? Who will draw a line from each house to each face? Are there as many houses as there are faces? How many faces are there? How many houses are there?

Continue in this manner, using a variety of combinations for the children to compare, count, and estimate.

To the Teacher. This activity should reinforce the child's understanding of the concept *as many as*. As they work with the objects, they must compare them. This can be done in a practical way by drawing imaginary lines to and from the groups of objects on the feltboard. In addition, they are reviewing the numbers one through six.

LET'S PLAY STORE!

Equipment. A table to use as the counter in a play store; toy cash register or money box; six pieces of play money; a selection of toys.

Procedure. ASK: Do you like to go shopping? What stores do you like best? Do you like to visit toy stores? Would you like to have a toy store right here?

SAY: Let's pretend that this table is the counter. We'll put lots of toys up here to sell. You can help me choose the toys. Do we have a cash register we could use at our store? Who would like to be storekeeper first?

Give each child some play money and let him buy a toy to play with for a while. Let the storekeeper determine how much the toy sells for—three dollars, two pennies, or whatever he chooses. Let the children count out the correct amount. Don't worry about having them differentiate between nickels and pennies or one-dollar bills and five-dollar bills. The object is to get them to count at least one through six items of money. Give each child a chance to be the storekeeper.

To the Teacher. The children will enjoy handling and counting the play money, choosing toys, and keeping store. As they participate in this activity, they are practicing their counting skills.

As early as 2000 B.C., the Chinese had a metallic form of currency, but not until 700 B.C. was a value fixed to a particular silver coin. This took place in Aegina, an island near Greece. Since that time, coins have been a major basis of trade and commerce.